50 WEIRDEST BIBLE STORIES

50 WEIRDEST BIBLE STORIES

Andy Robb

CWR

Copyright © Andy Robb, 2008

Published 2008 by CWR, Waverley Abbey House, Waverley Lane, Farnham, Surrey GU9 8EP, UK. Registered Charity No. 294387. Registered Limited Company No. 1990308. Reprinted 2009, 2010 (twice), 2011.

The right of Andy Robb to be identified as the author and illustrator of this work has been asserted by him in accordance with the Copyright, Designs and Patents Act 1988.

See back of book for list of National Distributors.

Editing, design and production by CWR

Cover image: Andy Robb

Printed in China by 1010 Printing.

ISBN: 978-1-85345-489-9

Intro

There are some things that are really difficult to do, such as eating jelly with a pair of chopsticks, not slurping through the straw when you get to the bottom of a milkshake and keeping a straight face when someone accidentally burps in the middle of quiet reading at school. But for most people, reading the Bible tops the lot of them.

If you've never so much as taken a sneaky peek between the covers of a Bible (and even if you have), it's sometimes really head-scratchingly tricky to know where exactly to begin. For starters, the Bible isn't one big book, it's lots of smaller books (sixty-six actually) that are all crammed together like a mini-library. The books have all got fancy names, such as Genesis (which is right at the very beginning), Job (pronounced JOBE), Psalms (pronounced SARMS), Mark (which you'll be relieved to know is actually pronounced MARK), Habakkuk (which should get you a pretty good score in a game of Scrabble) and Revelation (which is right at the very end).

Just to make it even more complicated, some of the books have got more than one section (like a sort of Part One and Part Two), and each Bible book doesn't just have chapters like normal books do, it has verses as well (like you get in poems).

So, if you wanted to have a read of chapter twenty and verse seven of the second book of Kings (cos there are two of them), you may find it written like this ...

2 Kings 20:7

... which, to me, looks more like a maths equation than anything to do with the Bible – but that's the way it is.

If you're itching to know what that Bible reference I just used is all about and also to find out how some perfectly good figs were (in my opinion) wasted, then you're going to need to get your hands on a copy of the Bible to check it out. In fact, you'll need a Bible to get the most out of this book so beg, borrow or buy yourself one as soon as you can.

As it's not always easy to decide which bit of the Bible to read first and in what order you should read it, we've gone and done all the hard work for you. Aren't we kind? In this book are fifty hand-picked Bible stories which are retold in a zappy style and with a colourful cartoon to stop you getting bored. At the end of each story you'll get the chance to find out what happens next (we don't tell you, you've got to do that for yourself – aren't we spoilsports?) and that's when you get to use your Bible. Using the info that we give you about where to find the story in the Bible, you'll need to look it up and then see how the story finishes. We've jumbled up the Old and New Testament stories, so remember the Old Testament all happened before Jesus came.

That's about it.

Happy reading and off you go!

MUD MAN

God's just finished creating the universe, paying particular attention to a rather tiddly planet called Earth. This place was going to be the apple of God's eye, so He'd filled it full to bursting with plants and vegetation and stuff. As His finishing touch, God made a creature that had exactly the same character traits as He did. Can you guess what it was called …? Yep, you've got it! Man. Just one itty-bitty problem. How do you make one? Good question.

Here's how God did it. He scooped up a handful of dirt from the ground and made a man out of it. Weird, perhaps, but you'll just have to take my word for it. But a lump of man-shaped clay, however good it might look, isn't much use to anybody, so God breathed into the man's nostrils and, kerbam! – the man came to life. Wow! Just in case you hadn't worked it out already, the world's first man was none other than Adam.

The Bible says that God thought that it would be a good idea if Adam had a best buddy, so God set His hand to doing a bit more clay modelling.

God made animals and birds of all shapes and sizes, but when push came to shove it soon became pretty obvious that none of them was going to be much good as a mate for our Adam.

So God set about His final creation and the icing on the cake. Woman. And here's the recipe God used. First take one man, preferably called Adam. Put him into a deep sleep. Take out one of his ribs (now you can see why he needed to be asleep). Last, but not least, use the rib to make a woman. Easy, huh? You'll no doubt have guessed who the world's first woman was. Yep, it was Eve.

One last thing. Can you think of something that God hasn't made for Adam and Eve that you think maybe they should have?

Hmm! Have a think about it then look up Bible book Genesis, chapter 2 and verse 25 for your answer.

2

GOD'S GRAFITTI

King Belshazzar of Babylon had got a bit too big for his boots and his great power had rather gone to his head. Never one to do things by halves, the king threw the mother of all parties for a thousand of his noblemen and their wives. As the finishing touch to his excesses, he gave orders for the wine to be served up in the gold cups and bowls that his dad (King Nebuchadnezzar) had nicked from God's Temple in Jerusalem. Bad move! As far as God was concerned, these things were special and most definitely not to be used in such a casual, couldn't-care-less sort of way. To make matters even worse, the revellers started to praise gods made of gold, silver, bronze, iron, wood and stone as they drank from the special cups and bowls. God was having none of that. To everyone's horror, a hand suddenly appeared (it was God) and began to write on the palace's plaster wall. The coloured drained from the king's face and his knees began to knock. He tentatively squinted through the half light to see what was written on the wall, but it made absolutely no sense to him whatsoever.

Belshazzar went into panic mode and shouted for his magicians, wizards and astrologers to tell him what the

writing meant. One by one, the royal advisers scratched their heads and tried to work out what on earth the scrawl on the wall said – but nothing doing. They were completely bamboozled.

Just in the nick of time, the queen mother turned up and said that she knew of a guy called Daniel who might just be able to help. From what she knew of Daniel, God seemed to have given him the ability to interpret dreams and understand mysterious stuff, such as strange writing on walls, so they fetched him, pronto.

Daniel said that God was telling Belshazzar He was calling time on his reign as a king because of his proud heart and his lack of respect for God.

Want to find out how long it took for Daniel's prediction to come true, then look up Bible book Daniel, chapter 5 and verses 30 and 31.

GOD'S GRUB

The Israelites were headed for a brand-new homeland (Canaan). After suffering at the hands of Egyptian slave masters for centuries you'd think that the Israelites would be a bit upbeat about being free. Not so! They were mega miffed about the meagre diet of food available to them in the desert they were crossing, and gave their leader (Moses) a right old ear-bashing about it.

God wasn't too happy about the way they were behaving and all it did was demonstrate their complete lack of trust in Him. Being the kind and generous God that He is, God gave Moses and his brother Aaron the lowdown on what He was going to do to fill the Israelites' bellies. First off, that very evening, the most ginormous flock of quails (nice, meaty birds) you've ever seen flew in and covered the camp. Let's hope the Israelites didn't stuff themselves silly because, next morning, breakfast turned up in the form of a thin, flaky substance which covered the desert floor like dew. It was as delicate as frost and sweet to taste. God had come good for them once again.

'What is it?' they asked, which is why it ended up getting called 'manna' which means, yes, you guessed it, 'What is it?'

God wanted to see if the grumbling Israelites really trusted Him so He told them that each person could collect up to two litres of manna a day, max, but nobody was allowed to stash any of the manna away until the next day. Some of them stupidly ignored this command, but tough luck – by the next day their manna was full of worms. Yuk! God had given the Israelites orders that, on the sixth day of the week, they were to collect twice as much manna so that it would last for the whole of the next day. Want to find out whether the manna that was kept over to the seventh day was full of worms?

Check it out in Bible book Exodus, chapter 16 and verse 24.

SNOOZE NEWS

Jacob had done a runner. He'd cheated on his older brother (Esau) and was scarpering as fast as his legs could carry him in the direction of his Uncle Laban's house in Mesopotamia. Jacob was next in line for heading up the Hebrew nation, but the way he felt at the moment there was no way he could see that ever happening.

One night at a place called Luz, he decided to rest his weary head and get some shut-eye. Not having a pillow handy, Jacob settled for the next best thing. A nice, hard rock. Hmm, sounds comfy! As Jacob slipped into the land of nod he began to have a weird dream. He could see a stairway stretching right up to heaven with angels going up and down it. Suddenly, in the dream, he saw God standing next to him. God told Jacob that he was going to give the land he was lying on (not just the bit with the pillow, silly, he meant the whole land) to his descendants, who'd be as numerous as the specks of dust in the earth. They'd extend their land in all directions and God was going to bless every other nation through them. To top it off, God promised Jacob that He'd never leave him and would always protect him.

Wow! What a dream. Jacob was so startled by it he woke up. Just the thought of knowing that God had been there sent shivers down his spine. It felt to him like he'd been sleeping at the doorway to heaven itself.

Not only had it been a weird experience for Jacob, it had also been a life-changing one, and he now needed to do something about it.

You can check out what he did for yourself in Bible book Genesis, chapter 28 and from verse 18 through to 22.

FLOCK SHOCK

I t's not much fun having a double-crossing uncle, but that was the lot of poor Jacob. Ever since he'd lived with his Uncle Laban and worked with his flocks they'd increased because God's blessing was on Jacob. Jacob had used his time well while he'd stayed there and had ended up marrying Laban's two daughters. Nice one, Jacob! Now he figured it was time to return to his homeland and it seemed only fair that he took with him some of Laban's flocks as payment. His uncle seemed OK with that, and just to avoid any misunderstanding, Jacob suggested that he only took the black lambs and the speckled and spotted goats. That way they'd both know what belonged to whom.

Seems fair enough. But while Jacob had his back turned, Laban's sons nicked all the black sheep and speckled and spotted goats and took them miles and miles away so that Jacob couldn't get his hands on them. What rotters!

Jacob wasn't gonna be outsmarted by his scheming uncle. He collected some green branches of poplar, almond and plane trees and stripped off some of the bark so that the branches had white stripes on them. Next up, he placed the branches in front of the remaining flocks' feeding trough, where the animals mated. Now for the weird bit. When the goats bred in front of the branches they gave birth to streaked, spotted and speckled young. How freaky is that?

There's one final twist to this weird story and you can find out what it is by looking up Bible book Genesis, chapter 30 and reading through verses 41 to 43.

DREAM ON

This Bible story stars a young man who I'm sure you're quite familiar with. His name is Joseph and you probably know him because of his amazing technicolour dreamcoat.

Sorry to have to disappoint you, but there was really nothing amazing about it and it certainly wasn't technicolour. It probably was ornate and colourful, if that's any good. Joseph's dad (Jacob) had made it especially for him (how kind) because Joe was the apple of his eye and the favourite out of all his twelve sons. For your info, they had four different mums in total so, with the exception of Benjamin (the youngest), they were actually his half-brothers. None of this exactly endeared Joseph to the rest of them. In fact, they gave him the cold shoulder and were generally quite off with him most of the time. So when Joseph had a weird dream about them all working in a corn field and their eleven sheaves of wheat forming a circle and bowing down to his, it didn't really go down too well. 'Do you think you are going to rule over us?' they chided him. After that they loathed him even more, if that was possible.

As if one dream wasn't enough to get their backs up, Joe then went and had another one.

Check out Bible book Genesis, chapter 37 and look up verses 9 through to 11. You'll also find out who else Joseph managed to rub up the wrong way with his dreams.

HIRE AND FIRE

Moses hardly had what you'd call a boring life. He'd been born into slavery in Egypt as an Israelite, become an Egyptian prince and was now living in the desert looking after his father-in-law's flocks. One day, when he was out and about with the sheep and goats, minding his own business, God showed up. When I say, showed up, what I mean is that He appeared to Moses in the form of a burning bush.

Moses didn't cotton on immediately that it was God. His first thoughts were probably why on earth the flaming bush wasn't burning up. After all, who'd ever heard of a fire-resistant bush? Weird or what? Moses only realised it was God when the bush started speaking to him. Ordinary bushes simply don't do that sort of thing.

As you can imagine, Moses was scared silly. God told him to take off his sandals because the place was now holy. Time to get down to business. God had a job for Moses to do even though Moses was getting on a bit (he was eighty years old). God's special nation (the Israelites) had been held as slaves in Egypt for hundreds of years and God had heard their cries for help.

The plan was for Moses to go and set them free. No big deal! Well, Moses thought it was. He was just a big nobody. Who was going to listen to an old-timer like him? God told Moses not to get so uptight. He'd do some stuff to convince Egypt's Pharaoh to let the Israelites go free. All Moses had to do was act as God's middleman.

Just to give Moses a little bit of extra encouragement, God told him how the story would end.

To find out how it did end you'll need to look up Bible book Exodus, chapter 3 and take a look at verses 21 to 22.

8
LIGHTS OUT

The Israelites were well cheesed off with being Egyptian slaves. They wanted out and God was doing His level best to free them from the clutches of nasty old Pharaoh, Egypt's ruler.

God's main man in all this was a guy called Moses. His job was to keep up the pressure on Pharaoh until he caved in. God's job was to show up in power so that Pharaoh realised that he couldn't win.

As we dive into this bit of the Bible story, God had already tightened the screws by inflicting the Egyptians with some pretty horrendous plagues, but Pharaoh was still digging his stubborn heels in and refusing to let the Israelites go. Time for God to serve up yet another pesky plague to convince Pharaoh to give in. God instructed Moses to raise his hand skyward, and, as he did, a thick darkness covered the land. The Bible says that it was so thick you could actually feel it. Weird! For three whole days the Egyptians couldn't see a thing. It was pitch black. How scary is that? As for the Israelites, well, it didn't affect the place where they lived. Double weird!

Pharaoh was finally getting ground down by all these plagues and he eventually agreed that the Israelites could go and worship God (a three-day journey into the desert) on one condition. They couldn't take their animals with them to sacrifice to God. Moses wasn't going to agree to that, and refused to negotiate.

What was Pharaoh's final answer? Go to Bible book Exodus, chapter 10 and verses 27 to 29 to find out if Pharaoh was still as stubborn as ever.

DOUBLE CROSSERS

Phew! The Israelites had finally been set free from slavery in Egypt and were heading to a new land God had lined up for them. Egypt's Pharaoh (their king) suddenly had second thoughts about losing all his slaves and decided that he wanted them back, pronto. He sent his army off in hot pursuit of the escaping Israelites, who'd camped by the Red Sea. When the Israelites saw the Egyptian chariots charging towards them they were scared witless. They put the blame squarely on Moses for bringing them out into the desert only to die. Moses tried his best to convince them that God was on their side and everything would be OK, but they didn't believe him.

Anyway, God already had something up His sleeve and He filled Moses in on His awesome plan. God told Moses to lift his wooden staff over the sea and, as he did, the weirdest thing happened. Before their very eyes the sea began to part. A pathway opened up through the sea with a whopper of a water wall on either side. To stop the Egyptians seeing what was happening, God sent a pillar of cloud to shut out all daylight from them but kept the Israelites in perfect daylight. The Israelites couldn't believe their eyes and they scurried across the pathway God had formed while the Egyptians gnashed their teeth in frustration, oblivious to what was happening on the other side of the cloud.

Want to find out what became of the Egyptian army? Check out Bible book Exodus, chapter 14 and have a look at verses 23 through to 28. It's a good read.

10
MOUNTAIN MEETING

It's always a bit nerve-wracking meeting someone for the first time, and even more so when that someone is none other than God. The Israelites had camped at the foot of Mount Sinai and Moses, their leader, was telling them what they needed to do so they'd make a good impression when God showed up in just three days' time. God expected them to be ritually clean as their Jewish religion taught them, and to get all spruced up with freshly washed clothes. And just in case they got any wrong notions of becoming too chummy with God, Moses marked a boundary line around the base of the mountain. If they even so much as set foot over that line they'd be put to death. Yikes! Moses warned them that they'd either be shot with an arrow or stoned. As far as God was concerned, His presence there made the place holy, and you don't mess around with God's holiness – end of story!

Sure enough, on the morning of Day Three, God began to make His grand entrance. The Israelites fixed their eyes on the mountain as they waited with bated breath for God to appear. A thick thunder cloud shrouded the mountain and flashes of lightning pierced the sky, followed by a weird and terrifying trumpet blast that just about scared the pants off

the lot of 'em. The Bible says that the whole of the mountain was covered in smoke like a furnace. God had come down onto the mountain in fire. As if that wasn't enough to get the Israelites' knocking knees working overtime, the trumpet blast got even louder and louder.

Being at the foot of the mountain was scary. Who in their right mind would want to cross over that boundary line even if God let them?

Well, take a look at Bible book Exodus, chapter 19, read verses 20 to 24 and you can find out.

MO GLOW

Rudolph the red-nosed reindeer might have had a shiny nose but he wasn't a patch on a guy called Moses. Moses headed up the Israelite nation and he often took time out to meet up with God and have a one-to-one with Him. It's a bit of a long story, but Moses has gone and broken two slabs of stone on which God had written some laws (which we call the Ten Commandments).

Moses is once again back up Mount Sinai, this time to collect a replacement pair of stone tablets from God. You and I know that if you spend time with anybody, something of them usually rubs off on you, and Moses' meet-ups with God were no exception. God is awesome, holy and powerful, so just being near Him does something to us. Moses spent a flabbergasting forty full days and nights (without food and water) up on the mountain with God, so no prizes for working out that something of God must have rubbed off on Israel's top man. When Moses finally came down from the mountain, the Bible tells us that his face was shining with a God-glow. You'd think that Moses' shiny face would be nice to look at but his brother, Aaron, and everyone else who saw him were freaked out by it and were afraid to go anywhere near him.

If you head to Bible book Exodus, chapter 34 and verse 33, you'll find how Moses solved this dilemma. Good thinking, Moses!

GIVE IT UP FOR GOD!

There's loads of stuff in the Bible about making sacrifices to God, and sometimes it seems a bit hard to get your head round. Before the Israelite nation had a land of their own to settle in they wandered round the desert, setting up camp for a bit until it was time to move on again. Wherever they went, a big tent called the tabernacle travelled with them. It was here that Israel's leaders met with God and it was here that sacrifices were made to Him.

All sorts of different sacrifices were made. A perfect whole animal was burnt to make up for their shortcomings. An offering of flour, baked cakes or grain was given as a way of making sure God saw the giver in a good light. The fat of an animal was burnt to keep God as your friend and the blood of an animal was sprinkled over the tabernacle to show that everything bad had been removed.

The job of looking after all these sacrifices was left to a bunch of guys called priests. It certainly couldn't be done by any old Tom, Dick or Harry. Everything had to be done in a very particular way, just as God had told them. This was really important. One wrong move and the sacrifice was as good as useless in God's eyes. One of the more famous priests was none

other than Moses' big bruvver, Aaron, and his first sacrifice was a nerve-wracking business. God warned him (and his sons who were helping) that if they put a foot wrong they'd be toast. Gulp! With great fear and trepidation they followed God's instructions to the letter. At long last their first sacrifice was done and they were still alive. What a relief!

That's when the weirdest of things happened.

To find out what it was you're going to need to look up Bible book Leviticus, chapter 9 and check out verses 22 through to 24. It's hot stuff!

FANGS A LOT!

It wasn't much fun for the Israelites roaming to and fro across the desert before God allowed them to enter a new land He'd lined up. Why the long wait? God was waiting for all the moaners and groaners who'd rebelled against Him to pop their clogs (die) before He did let them in. But, sad to say, they were still grumbling and muttering, even after all God had done for them.

Given half a chance they'd probably shoot back to Egypt where they'd been slaves. The ungrateful Israelites figured that it would at least be better than wandering about in the desert feeling hungry and thirsty. To be fair to God, He gave the Israelites food day in, day out, but even that wasn't enough for them. They were getting bored of eating the same stuff all the time. Why couldn't God change the menu? God was having none of their back chat. He'd had a bellyful of their complaining and His patience had finally run out. God sent a plague of slimy snakes into the Israelite camp. As you can imagine, loads of the Israelites got bitten by the snakes and died. That soon stopped their griping.

The Israelites realised what a clanger they'd made with all their grumbling and asked Moses, ever so nicely, if he could pray to God to get rid of those mean and nasty killer snakes – pretty please! Moses duly obliged and God told him how to stop the slaughter. He was to make a metal snake and stick it on a pole. Weird or what!

What was Moses supposed to do with that? Hit the snakes? Nope, but if you want to find out, go to Bible book Numbers, chapter 21 and take a look at verses 8 and 9.

WATER MIRACLE!

Moses, the leader of the Israelite nation, was a bit of a hard act to follow, but Joshua (his successor) was giving it his best shot. The entire nation was getting itself ready to enter the land of Canaan which God had given them to live in. Just one niggling problem that looked like it was going to put a downer on the whole thing. The Jordan River was in the way. As if that wasn't enough, right at that very moment it was also in full flood. Just what they needed! This looked like it was gonna be make or break time for Joshua.

Fortunately for our Josh, God was on his side and had already told him how they were going to do the seemingly impossible. Here's how. For three days the Israelites were to get themselves ready and then, when it was time to get moving, the priests were to lead the way, carrying a special box called the ark of the covenant. It represented God being with them. The people were told to keep at a good distance from the priests and wait to see what they did. When the priests finally reached the water's edge, something weird happened. As they dipped their toes into the swollen river it suddenly stopped flowing. It was if somebody had turned the tap off somewhere up river. Actually, that wasn't too

far from the truth. Further upstream, at a place called
Adam, the water simply piled up in a heap.
Difficult to get your head round,
I know, but that's
the way it was.

To discover the end to this
fascinating Bible story
you'll need to look it up in
Bible book Joshua, chapter
3 and verse 17.

PARK ARK

srael's arch enemy (the Philistines) had captured its most treasured possession, the ark of the covenant. This was an ornate box with some special things inside it that showed that God was with the Israelites.

Foolishly, the Philistines stored the ark in the temple of their god, Dagon, in a place called Ashdod. Next morning, the people of the city discovered that the statue of their god had come crashing down during the night in front of the special box. How weird. They set the statue back upright, but the next morning the same thing had happened again and this time the statue was in pieces. Weirder still.

The penny suddenly dropped that God was not happy with them. Just to make sure they got the message that you don't mess with God, He sent a plague of tumours to afflict the people of the region. Panic stations! The five Philistine kings had an urgent conflab and decided to move the ark somewhere else.

They moved it to a place called Gath, but as soon as it arrived a plague of tumours broke out there as well. The people were terrified. So, they moved the ark yet again, this time to Ekron. No prizes for guessing what happened next.

Yep, you're right. A plague of tumours broke out there. By now the Philistines were at their wits' end. What were they to do? It was their magicians who finally put two and two together and suggested returning the ark to Israel, ASAP (as soon as possible). They figured that it might also help if they sent it back with a gift.

What did they have in mind? A box of chocs? Some flowers? A gift token? Nope – five gold models of tumours and five gold mice. How thoughtful!

The ark eventually showed up at the Israelite town of Beth Shemesh, but some of the men of the town made a big mistake. You can find out what it was by going to Bible book 1 Samuel, chapter 6 and reading verse 19.

16
SAUL THE FOOL

Things weren't going well for King Saul of Israel. He'd made a right old pig's ear of ruling God's special nation and God wanted nothing more to do with him. Israel's No.1 enemy (the Philistines) were getting ready to attack them and Saul was petrified. He desperately tried to contact God to find out what to do but the line was dead. To make matters worse, Samuel, the great prophet of God who used to give Saul good advice, was dead as well. What a predicament!

Then Saul struck upon a daft idea. He decided to consult a medium, which is someone who is supposedly able to contact the dead. What's even more bizarre is that the king had just chucked all the mediums and fortunetellers out of Israel because God hated what they did. Make your mind up, Saul.

Saul eventually managed to track down a medium at a place called Endor. At the dead of night, he paid her a surprise visit (dressed in a disguise so that he wouldn't be recognised) and told the medium to contact Samuel. Maybe he could help him from beyond the grave. The woman thought that he was trying to trick her because the king had banished all mediums, and she was even more concerned when she found out it was the king himself who was speaking to her.

The medium did her spooky stuff and summoned the spirit of Samuel who showed up wearing a cloak. He was not at all pleased with Saul for disturbing him. In fact, Samuel gave the king a piece of his mind before he disappeared.

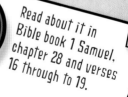

Read about it in Bible book 1 Samuel, chapter 28 and verses 16 through to 19.

17 MIRACLE MEAL

Elijah the prophet had hot-footed it as fast as his legs could carry him in the opposite direction of wicked King Ahab and his equally wicked wife, Jezebel. Elijah had commanded there to be a drought over the land of Israel and now he was in bad King Ahab's bad books for it.

God had told Elijah to head to the brook of Cherith where there was water to drink. That was great but what about food? No problem. God sent him bread and meat as regular as clockwork, delivered by ravens. Yes, you heard me – ravens. When the brook eventually dried up (because there was no rain) God had another clever plan to keep Elijah fed and watered. He told Elijah to head for the town of Zarepath and to go to the house of a widow who'd take care of him.

When Elijah turned up, things didn't look too good. The poor widow was just getting ready to cook one last meal for herself and her son before they got ready to die of starvation. All she had left in the whole wide world was a measly handful of flour in a bowl and a drop of olive oil at the bottom of a jar. There was no way that Elijah was going to get fat on that.

Now here's the weird part. The prophet told her to quit fretting and to bake a small loaf of bread for them, which she

did. Elijah promised the widow (on God's authority) that the flour and the oil wouldn't run out until God sent rain to end the drought.

Was he telling the truth? You'll need to check this one out by looking up Bible book 1 Kings, chapter 17 and verses 15 and 16.

DISAPPEARING ACT

Enoch and Elijah (who both feature in the Bible) had one thing in common. Neither of them actually died. Weird as you might think it, the pair of them simply went straight up to heaven when their time was up on planet Earth. That's what I call style! Anyway, this story is about Elijah and how it happened for him.

Elijah knew that his time was almost up and so he'd packed his bags and set off on his final journey. Elisha (his apprentice) stuck to him like glue and wouldn't let Elijah out of his sight. When they got to Bethel, a bunch of prophets told Elisha what was going to happen to his master but he didn't want to talk about it. Probably too upset. Next stop was Jericho and there the same thing happened again with another bunch of prophets. Elisha didn't want to be told by them either that Elijah was about to shoot off to heaven.

Last stop was the River Jordan, where Elijah coolly struck the water with his rolled up cloak and it parted before their very eyes. The pair of prophets crossed over to the other side, but before Elijah disappeared from his life forever, Elisha wanted some of his master's super-duper power. Here's

the deal Elijah offered him. If Elisha witnessed him being whisked off to heaven, the power was his. You couldn't say fairer than that.

Want to read about Elijah's dramatic exit from this world? Flick through to Bible book 2 Kings, chapter 2 and take a look at verses 11 and 12. Exciting stuff!

PROPHET AND LOSS

Whenever he passed through the town of Shunem, Elisha (one of God's prophets) stayed at the home of a rich lady and her hubbie. Being a generous couple they even gave this mighty man of God his own cosy, rooftop room. Elisha wanted to repay their kindness and found out from his servant (Gehazi) that the couple had no son and it looked like it was going to stay that way because the husband was well past his sell-by date.

Elisha wasn't fazed by this and told the woman that, in a year's time, she'd be the proud mum of a baby boy. To be perfectly honest she thought Elisha was kidding, but he wasn't and it happened just as he had said.

Fast-forwarding a few years, we catch up with the lad as he's out in the fields gathering in the harvest. All of a sudden he complained of pains in his head and before they knew it he was stone dead. The boy's mum was distraught but she knew that if she could just get hold of Elisha, he'd be able to do something. She saddled up her donkey and raced off to find him. Elisha sent Gehazi off ahead of them with instructions to hold his wooden stick over the boy. He did as his master had directed but nothing doing. The lad was still cold and lifeless. So Elisha did something even weirder than holding a stick over the boy's head.

You can read about it in Bible book 2 Kings, chapter 4 and verses 32 through to 37 to see if it had any more success.

LETHAL LUNCH

If you like watching cookery programmes on the telly then you'll love this Bible story. While Elisha was doing a spot of teaching to a bunch of prophets, his servant toddled off to knock up some lunch. Elisha fancied stew, so the servant went off into the fields to see what yummy ingredients he could find to bung in it. He stumbled across a wild vine and picked as many gourds as he could possibly carry. Once he'd sliced them up, he popped them into the boiling pot. Just one problem. The servant hadn't a clue what they were. Were the gourds poisonous or were they safe to eat? Hmm, good question!

When it was time for grub up, the peckish prophets started tucking into their dinner. But not for long. 'It's poisoned!' they told Elisha. He quickly grabbed a handful of meal, flung it into the pot and told them the panic was now off, it was OK to eat.

Another weird food story occurred when a guy showed up with twenty barley loaves. The plan was to use them to feed Elisha and the hundred or so prophets who were hanging out with him. As far as Elisha's servants were concerned there was no way that twenty loaves were going to feed a big crowd of hungry men. Or would they?

Have a look at Bible book 2 Kings, chapter 4 and verses 43 to 44 for your answer.

A BIT OF A BAD JOB

ancy hearing about the hard luck story to beat all hard luck stories? Here goes. There was this guy from Uz called Job (but pronounced Jobe) who worshipped God and was an all round jolly good chap. He had ten kids, thousands of sheep, camels, cattle, donkeys and servants and was (according to the Bible) the richest man in the East. Unfortunately for Job, Satan (God's enemy) had his eye on him and reckoned that without his wealth he wouldn't be such a godly guy. So God allowed Satan to put Job through the wringer and to see what he was made of.

The first disaster to befall Job was that every last animal of his was either stolen or killed. Before Job even had a chance to get to grips with the scale of his loss, a servant raced in with the terrible news that all his kids had been killed when the house they were in was destroyed by a gale. The final straw came when Job was afflicted by a horrid disease that covered him in sores from head to toe.

Amazingly, despite these terrible setbacks, Job continued to praise God. Job had three best buddies (Eliphaz, Bildad and Zophar) who dropped by to comfort the poor fella. They tried their level best to convince their best buddy that the troubles he was going through were his fault, but Job would have none of it. His wife even chipped in and tried to persuade Job to curse God, but to his credit he wouldn't.

Did Job's story have a happy ending? Head for Bible book Job, chapter 42 and check out verses 10 through to 16 for your answer. If you fancy an extra bit of detective work, look at verse 5 to see how Job's terrible trials changed his life.

FIERY FELLAS

King Nebuchadnezzar of Babylon reckoned himself – big time. He even went as far as to have a huge gold statue of himself built, and anybody who didn't worship it was for the chop. Three guys who didn't play ball were Shadrach, Meshach and Abednego. They were Jews and worshipped the Lord God Almighty.

Nothing was going to make this tenacious trio bow the knee to a lump of gold. For your info, the king was absolutely livid and gave the command for them to be flung into the furnace, pronto. Nebuchadnezzar was so teeth-gnashingly mad, he had the heat turned up until it was seven times hotter than usual. Shadrach, Meshach and Abednego were tied up and thrown headlong into the fiery furnace. It was so hot that the men who chucked them in got burned to a cinder in the process.

As the king looked on with eager anticipation, waiting to see his three rebellious subjects barbecued to a crisp, his jaw dropped in utter amazement. Of all the weird things, he could see the men walking around inside the furnace – but there weren't three of them, there were four! Not only that, but none of them was burnt. What was going on?

He commanded the men to come out of the fire, and Shadrach, Meshach and Abednego did. Nebuchadnezzar looked them up and down. The fire hadn't touched them. Their clothes weren't burnt, their hair wasn't singed and they didn't even smell of smoke.

Want to find out how this weird experience affected that proud king? Have a look at Bible book Daniel, chapter 3 and verses 28 to 30.

23

HEAVENLY HUBBUB

Most people have got their own ideas of what God looks like but the fact is, nobody really knows. Isaiah was a prophet of God who lived in Jerusalem long, long ago, and he had a vision of God that just about blew him away. If it had been for real it would probably have killed the guy.

In his vision, Isaiah saw God on His throne, in His Temple and dressed in a robe that completely swamped the place. God was surrounded by weird and wonderful six-winged creatures who kept calling out to each other about how holy God was. I'll tell you something for nothing, heaven (where God lives) is nothing like some of the churches you come across which are so quiet you could just about hear a pin drop. The awesome creatures that Isaiah clapped his eyes on made so much noise the very foundations of the Temple shook. Wow! Isaiah was completely overwhelmed. In comparison with God's holiness he felt dirty. Suddenly, one of the winged creatures flew towards him and touched his lips with a red-hot lump of coal. Ouch! In an instant Isaiah knew that all the grot in his life had gone.

God hadn't quite finished with Isaiah yet. God's voice could be heard asking who He could send as His messenger.

Without hesitation, Isaiah said that he was up for it. He'd be God's mouthpiece. And that's how Isaiah got the job of telling the people of Judah what God had to say to them. Just for your info, Isaiah has a massive sixty-six chapters of the Bible all to himself. One of the most famous things he had to say is read out at Christmas and was God's way of announcing that He was going to send Jesus to planet Earth and the unusual nature of His birth.

To find out what I'm talking about, go to Bible book Isaiah, chapter 7 and verse 14.

24

UNHAPPY FAMILIES

When it comes to having patience, God wins hands down. If you and I were God (which we're not) we'd have given up on the human race ages ago.

This Bible story features a guy called Hosea who'd got the unenviable task of telling the people of Israel what a rotten lot they were. God expected them to be faithful to Him, just as He'd been faithful to them, but they really couldn't have cared less. Instead of just worshipping the God who'd given life to their nation in the first place, they chose to worship a right old mixed bag of idols and gods. God planned to let them know how unfaithful they'd been, which is where poor, unfortunate Hosea comes in.

God told Hosea to get himself a wife but, and here's the weird bit, he had to make sure she was unfaithful. How odd is that? Gomer was her name and she certainly came up trumps when it came to being unfaithful. Hosea must have been heartbroken, which is exactly what God wanted the people of Israel to understand. That's how He felt, being cheated on by them.

It wasn't just Hosea's wife whom God used to speak to Israel. He used Hosea's kids as well. Take a look at Bible book Hosea, chapter 1 and check out verses 3 through to 7.

25

MEGA MATES

Jesus did some pretty unconventional things in His time, no more so than this weird and wonderful way of healing a paralysed man. Just to set the scene, Jesus was visiting a place called Capernaum and word soon got out that He was in town. Whenever Jesus showed up, miracles seemed to happen and everyone seemed to want a slice of the action. Jesus was holed up in a house, teaching the crowds about God.

The place was positively heaving and it was standing room only. Four men turned up with their sick friend. They were desperate for Jesus to heal him. He was paralysed and without their help he stood no chance. Seeing that there was no way in through the crushing crowds they climbed up to the top of the house, cleared a hole in the roof, and lowered their sick pal down right in front of Jesus. The Bible says that Jesus was well impressed with their faith that He could heal their friend. He looked the sick man in the eyes, and instead of placing His hands on his body, He simply told the guy that his sins were forgiven.

That sure didn't go down well with the religious leaders in the crowd. As far as they were concerned it was only God who forgave people. If Jesus was making Himself

out to be God (which He was) then that was blasphemy.
Jesus (because He was God) knew full well what they were
thinking and bluntly told the disgruntled religious leaders
that this was the very point
He was making. He
wanted everyone to see
that He was God.

Did the man get better?
Find out by looking up Bible
book Mark, chapter 2 and
verses 10 through to 12.

26

WATER NIGHT!

I t had been a busy old day for Jesus and He really needed a bit of time out to recharge His batteries. He sent His disciples on ahead of Him to the other side of Lake Galilee and then climbed up a hill to pray.

As night drew in and the disciples were well out into the lake, the wind started to whip up. A storm was brewing out on the open sea and their small sailing boat was getting tossed all over the place. Sometime between three and six in the morning, the disciples looked out onto the surging sea and saw the weirdest of things. It was Jesus, but He wasn't in a boat. He was walking towards them on the water. The Bible says that they were terrified, and wouldn't you be?

Jesus tried to calm their thumping hearts and reassure them. Then Peter, the most impulsive of the bunch, chipped in. He wanted a bit more convincing that this really was Jesus. 'Lord, if it is really You, tell me to come out on the water to You.' Did Peter know what he was saying? Jesus took him at his word and called him over. Without a second thought Peter climbed over the side of the boat and started walking towards Jesus. Just when it looked like he was going to make it, Peter got freaked by the howling wind and started to sink like a stone.

Did Peter end his days in a watery grave? Discover the answer in Bible book Matthew, chapter 14 and verses 31 and 32.

27

MOUNTAIN MYSTERY

I wonder if Jesus included 'climbing mountains' in the job description when He was picking His disciples (the bunch of guys who helped Him do His stuff)? Israel had loads of mountains and hills and Jesus often climbed them to speak to the crowds below. It was much easier that way. Jesus also liked escaping to the mountains to take time out with God, and that's where we catch up with Him in this particular Bible story.

Also along for the outing were Peter, James and John, three of Jesus' best buddies. When they were completely alone, out of sight of the clamouring crowds, something weird happened to Jesus. His appearance began to change and His clothes became dazzling white. Whiter than the whitest wash from your washing machine, in fact whiter than anything you've ever seen in your life. If that wasn't enough to flabbergast the awestruck threesome, try this for size. Two famous (and long dead) guys from the Bible (Moses and Elijah) showed up. What a day this was turning out to be. Peter had ants in his pants and in his excitement and bewilderment suggested that maybe they should make three tents. One for Jesus, one for Moses and one for Elijah.

As if there weren't enough weird happenings for one day, a cloud suddenly appeared and eclipsed them with its shadow. Just when they thought that they couldn't take any more surprises, God's voice boomed out from the cloud. 'This is my own dear Son. Listen to Him!' Jesus' mates quickly looked about them but the only person they could see was Jesus. I'm guessing that the three of them couldn't wait to spill the beans and to tell all and sundry what they'd seen and heard.

Did they? Find out what Jesus had to say on the matter in Bible book Mark, chapter 9 and verse 9.

28

A DUMB THING TO SAY

The job of looking after God's Temple in Jerusalem was down to a bunch of guys called priests. One of them (Zechariah) was about to get the surprise of his life. He showed up for work as normal and got stuck into doing the usual priest-type things, like burning incense on the altar (inside the Temple) while everybody else hung around outside praying.

Without a word of warning, a bright, shiny angel appeared and scared him half to death. Once the angel had got Zechariah breathing normally and his heart rate down, he gave him the good news that his wife (Elizabeth) was going to have a baby boy called John. Not only that but he was going to be a special kid who, when he grew up, would be part of God's plan to get their nation (Israel) back to being friends with Him. Zech was bowled over. Just one thing though. Zechariah and his good lady wife were getting on a bit, not to put too fine a point on it. As far as Zech could see there was absolutely no way that a decrepit old couple like them were ever going to have a baby. Not at their age. That would be weird! Zechariah figured that God had made a mistake and he said as much to the angel. Bad move! Because Zechariah had disbelieved the angel he was struck dumb until the baby was born.

Did Zech get his voice back? Find out by taking a look in Bible book Luke, chapter 1 and have a read of verses 57 through to 66.

29

DEAD CLEVER

Almost everywhere Jesus went, large crowds followed Him. People were desperate for Him to touch them so they would be healed. Jairus was in charge of a synagogue, which made him a pretty important chap, but that didn't stop him barging his way through the crowds and falling at Jesus' feet to beg Him to heal his dying daughter. He figured that Jesus was his last chance. He was convinced that if only Jesus could place His hands on the girl she'd live. So Jesus followed Jairus to his house.

Sadly, before they got there Jairus' servants came out to meet him, bearing the bad news that his daughter was a goner. Amazingly, Jesus completely blanked them and simply told Jairus to keep on believing.

When they arrived at Jairus' house the place was full of mourners, weeping and wailing at the top of their voices. What a din! Jesus wanted to know what all the fuss was about. He told them that the girl wasn't dead, just asleep. They thought He was stark raving mad and laughed at Him. Jesus cleared them all out of the house and then headed off to see the girl with three of His disciples and Jairus and his wife in tow.

Taking the dead girl by the hand, Jesus told her to get up. That was it. No fancy stuff, just a couple of words. I'll bet you're itching to know if she did come back to life again, aren't you?

Go to Bible book Mark, chapter 5 and verse 42 to find out.

30

GUESS THE GUEST

ere's what's been happening. Three days had passed since Jesus had been executed by the Romans and rumours were now flying around that He'd actually come back to life. Weird or what? When He was alive Jesus had loads of people following Him round, watching what He did and hanging on His every word. A couple of these people, who may have been husband and wife, were on their way to the village of Emmaus and were passing the time by having a bit of a chinwag about Jesus and everything that had recently happened to Him. Out of nowhere, Jesus Himself joined the travelling twosome, but it was weird. Somehow they didn't quite twig that it was Him.

Jesus asked what they were chatting about. They couldn't quite believe that He hadn't a clue what had been going on in Jerusalem, but Jesus was just playing dumb so He could hear their take on things. The two started to fill Him in on how the religious leaders had got it in for Jesus and how the Romans had done their dirty work for them by crucifying the Man they hoped would rescue Israel. As Emmaus came into view, Jesus made as if He was going to keep on going, but the pair persuaded Him to stop over with them for the night.

It wasn't until dinner time that they suddenly worked out who their travelling companion was. Here's how they figured it out. The night before He died, Jesus had one last meal with His disciples at which He'd broken a loaf of bread to show them how His life was going to be given for them. Jesus did the self same thing at this meal, at which point the hosts immediately realised the Man eating with them was Jesus come back to life again.

Want to find out if Jesus stayed for dessert? If so, you're going to need to look in Bible book Luke, chapter 24 and verse 31.

31

SHOW TIME

Some people believe in ghosts and get scared at even the thought of them, but when Jesus started to pop up all over the place (soon after He'd died) there certainly wasn't anything spooky about it. Before Jesus had died and gone back to heaven (where He'd come from) He told His closest friends that being executed by the Romans wasn't going to be the end of Him, and guess what, He was right. Against all the odds God miraculously brought Jesus back to life.

The first to discover this were three women who'd come to pay their respects at Jesus' tomb. It didn't take them long to find out that not only was Jesus not inside it any more, but, even weirder, He was slap-bang in front of one them, chatting away as if nothing had happened.

That was just the beginning. Jesus' next surprise appearance was to some of His disciples who were holed up in a locked room. Jesus didn't bother with knocking on the door. He just showed up in the middle of them. They were blown away to realise that this same Jesus whom they'd seen breathe His last a few days earlier, was now very much alive and kicking.

Jesus showed up again a week later to make a personal visit to Thomas, who'd missed out first time round. Thomas said that

he wasn't going to be convinced that it really was Jesus until he touched the holes in Jesus' flesh where He'd been nailed to a wooden cross to die. As soon as he did so, he believed.

Yet another time, Jesus rustled up a beach barbecue of bread and fish for His disciples after they returned from a fishing trip. How kind was that? Jesus was popping up all over the place making sure everybody got the message that He'd beaten death and that God had made it possible for everyone to get to know Him because of it.

One last thing. Check out Bible book 1 Corinthians, chapter 15 and verse 6 to read up on the biggest sighting of Jesus (back from the dead) that's recorded.

32

WE HAVE LIFT-OFF!

Once Jesus had finished His mighty mission to make it possible for us to be friends with God, it was time for Him to go home to heaven. Jesus' tip-top team (His disciples) were trained up and ready to carry on where He left off. But one thing's for sure, you can't catch a flight to heaven, so Jesus' departure lounge was the next best thing – a mountain near Bethany. His disciples had been instructed to meet Him there, though who knows if they had any idea of the weird events they were about to witness. Probably not!

First off, Jesus reminded this crack team that their job (once He'd gone) was to tell anybody and everybody that they needed to believe that Jesus was God's Son and the only Person who could guarantee them a one-way ticket to heaven. Their job spec also included baptising people, healing the sick and getting rid of evil spirits. In fact, all the stuff that Jesus had been doing.

Jesus and His motley crew had become a tight-knit team over the three years they'd spent living and working together, but it was now time to say their fond farewells. Jesus blessed them, lifted up His hands to heaven and then simply disappeared up into the sky. That was it! He was gone.

Would they ever see their Lord again? You're going to have to read Bible book Acts, chapter 1 and verses 10 and 11 if you want to find out the answer to that.

33

REAL HEAL

Jesus was in His home town of Capernaum and the place was positively heaving with people who'd turned out see Him. Just imagine a TV celebrity showing up in your hometown and you've sort of got the picture of what it was like. Some folk had showed up cos they were desperate to get Jesus to heal them and others were probably just plain old nosey and wanted to catch a glimpse of this famous Man of God. Either way, you couldn't move for people.

Right in the thick of it was a sick lady who'd suffered from a terrible bleeding condition for a dozen or so years. She'd spent all her cash on doctors but they were a complete waste of time and money. They couldn't do a thing to help her and she was now at her wits' end. When she heard that Jesus was in town, the lady knew that He was her last chance to get well again. If He couldn't heal her then nobody could.

She pushed her way through the chaotic crowd until she came within arms' reach of Jesus. It was now or never. She reached out and touched the edge of Jesus' cloak and the bleeding stopped – just like that!

But here's the weird thing. Jesus wanted to know who'd touched Him. Come off it! You couldn't move for people and yet Jesus wanted to know who'd touched Him. That's ridiculous, isn't it? Nope. Well, at least not according to Jesus. He told Peter (one of His disciples) that power had gone out of Him because someone had touched Him.

The woman who'd been healed knew that she'd been rumbled and came clean. In fear and trepidation she confessed what she'd done.

Was Jesus mad? Find out in Bible book Luke, chapter 8 and verse 48. You'll also discover the key to her getting healed.

34

ROAD RUNNER

ere's a weird Bible story to get your teeth into. It kicks off with a follower of Jesus called Philip who was going great guns for God in a place called Samaria. Miracles were happening all over the place and it looked like he'd be there for ages because God was using him so powerfully.

Not so! An angel showed up and told Philip to pack his bags and to head off in a certain direction, which he dutifully did. Faithful Phil hot-footed it to the old road that ran from Jerusalem to Gaza. Just as he arrived a posh carriage came into view. Inside sat one of the Queen of Ethiopia's main men, on his way back from worshipping God in Jerusalem. Time for our Phil's next instruction. The Holy Spirit told him to hurry over to the carriage and stick close to it. As Philip jogged alongside it he could hear its occupant reading from the book of the prophet Isaiah. Hey, this looked promising. Philip asked the Ethiopian if he had any idea what the stuff he was reading meant. The guy hadn't a clue so Phil filled him in. He climbed on board, took a seat and launched into telling the VIP next to him that the Bible bit was all about Jesus and how Jesus had died to take the punishment for all

the things we do wrong and how anyone can get to know God because of Jesus. The Ethiopian wanted to become a follower of Jesus. He jumped down from the carriage and got Philip to baptise him by the roadside.

Now for the weird bit, but you're going to have to look this up for yourself in Bible book Acts, chapter 8 and verses 38 through to 40. You'll be amazed!

35

CRUEL SAUL

Saul, if you've never heard of the guy before (not King Saul), was a big-time Bible baddy. Boo! Hiss! Saul got his kicks from hating anybody who followed Jesus and he spent all his spare time making their life an absolute misery. He'd been involved in the murder of one of them, a guy called Stephen (who'd been stoned to death) and he'd tried his level best to completely wipe out the Church, going from house to house, dragging out believers in Jesus and flinging them into jail. Saul was the original Mr Nasty, but all of that was about to change.

Saul was on his way to Damascus to do more dastardly deeds when he was stopped in his tracks by a bright light that flashed around him. As he collapsed on the ground in a heap, a voice called out to him. It was none other than Jesus. He wanted to know why Saul was giving Him such a hard time, but Saul didn't have an answer. Jesus told Saul to finish his journey to Damascus where He'd tell him what to do next.

When Saul opened his eyes he couldn't see a thing. He was as blind as a bat and had to be led the rest of the way by his travelling companions. He didn't eat or drink a thing for the next three days until a man called Ananias showed up and said that God had sent him with a message for Saul.

If you want to discover what the message was, then head for Bible book Acts, chapter 9 and read verses 17 to 19.

36

JAILHOUSE ROCKED

oing stuff for God can be a right old risky business, as Paul and Silas soon found out in a place called Philippi. They'd set a slave girl free from an evil spirit that helped her tell the future, and which made pots of money for her owners. The owners were well miffed and had the pair arrested as trouble-makers by the Roman rulers.

After a good old flogging, Paul and Silas were banged up in prison, and just to make sure they didn't do a runner, their feet were fastened between heavy blocks of wood. Were Paul and Silas bovverd? No way! The Bible says that, at around midnight, they were having a sing-song to God and praying. I'll bet the other prisoners thought they were off their rockers.

But suddenly the weirdest thing happened. The prison was shaken to its foundations by a whopping great earthquake. All the doors flew open and the chains fell off the prisoners. The jailer was horrified. He thought that everyone had escaped and was about to kill himself when Paul stopped him in his tracks. Everyone was accounted for – none of the prisoners had scarpered.

The jailer fell at Paul's feet. It was plain to him that God

had caused the earthquake and he was shaking in his boots.
He wanted to know what he needed to do to get into
God's good books. 'Believe in the Lord
Jesus,' Paul told him, 'it's
as simple as that.'

Did the jailer take Paul's
advice? Check out Bible
book Acts, chapter 16 and
read verses 32 through to
34 for your answer.

37

SHIVER AND SNAKE

How do you fancy being shipwrecked? Me neither. Well, Paul, the star of this Bible story, had to put up with being shipwrecked not once but three times. We catch up with the poor fella as he's just been washed ashore on the Mediterranean island of Malta after enduring a couple of weeks at sea (in a boat) being tossed around by a ferocious storm.

The Maltese people came to the rescue and took care of the survivors. As if they weren't wet enough already, it then started to tip it down with rain. A fire was lit to warm them all up and Paul lent a hand collecting firewood. As he flung it on the fire a startled snake (which had been disturbed by the heat) shot out from the undergrowth. It sunk its ferocious fangs into Paul's hand. Ouch! As the slippery fiend dangled from Paul's hand, the islanders started to ask themselves if this was perhaps him getting his come-uppance for being a murderer or something like that.

Whatever they thought, they were wrong. Did Paul keel over and die? He didn't. Paul just shook the snake off into the sea with absolutely zero ill effects. How weird is that?

The natives then had second thoughts and came to the

conclusion that Paul must therefore be a god instead. That was wrong as well. The truth was that God had protected Paul because he trusted in Him.

Want to see how Paul passed his time at Malta? Take a look in Bible book Acts, chapter 28 and verses 7 through to 10.

38

FIG TREE FAITH

Jesus was on His way to Jerusalem after a stopover in nearby Bethany. His disciples had spent three years of their life with Him and they still didn't completely understand everything He did or said, and today was going to be another one of those days.

The Bible tells us that Jesus was a wee bit peckish, so when He saw a fig tree up ahead He made a beeline for it. When He got there He was miffed to discover there wasn't a fig to be found. What good is a fig tree without figs? Jesus said that nobody would ever eat figs from the tree again. It was final. OK, so it sounds a bit harsh, but Jesus was actually using this to show what a bad job Israel's religious leaders had made of things. God had expected them to help people to know Him and to live lives that pleased Him but, like the fig tree, they had produced little or no fruit.

The very next day, as Jesus and His disciples passed that same way again, one of them did a bit of a double take. Peter couldn't believe his eyes. He pointed out to Jesus that the fig tree that He'd cursed the previous day was dead, right down to its roots. Even more astounding, though, is the promise that Jesus gave them after this weird and wonderful event.

You can find out what this promise is by looking up Bible book Mark, chapter 11 and verses 22 to 24, and then ask yourself the question, What am I going to do with this promise?

39

TEMPLE TURMOIL

If you know a thing or two about Jesus you probably know all about the time He arrived in Jerusalem (on a colt) and people spread palm branches on the ground, hollering 'Hosanna to the Son of David' at the tops of their voices to welcome Him. Do you want to know what happened right after that? Well, let me tell you.

Next up, Jesus made a beeline for Jerusalem's Temple where people came to bring their sacrifices to God. The Temple was the centre of Jewish life and a mega important building for both the Jews and for God. If Jesus was expecting the place to be shipshape and as God expected it to be then He had another think coming. Jesus was shocked by the sight that met His eyes. Jews had to pay a Temple tax but it had to be paid with Temple currency, so the Temple had attracted cheating money changers who were charging people over the odds to change up their cash. That was a big no-no as far as Jesus was concerned. Added to which, the place was also heaving with cattle and people selling doves to be sacrificed to God. What had happened to the peaceful and special place the Temple was supposed to be? It had been turned into little more than

a market and Jesus was livid that it wasn't being treated with respect. Rather than politely asking the traders to shut up shop, Jesus went wild. He overturned their tables and drove out the traders with a whip.

Did Jesus then do a runner before the market traders turned on him? Check out Bible book Mark, chapter 11 and verses 16 and 17 to find out.

40

WIFE STRIFE

Abraham was best mates with God but he still sometimes made a bit of a mess of things. For instance, there was the time he was travelling through Gerar in Canaan. Although Abraham trusted God to look after him, he wasn't too sure about King Abimelech who ruled the roost round those parts. Abraham's wife (Sarah) was a bit of a good-looking lass and Abraham was worried that the king might nick her and make Sarah his wife instead. The plan Abraham hatched was to say that Sarah was his sister (she was, in fact, his half-sister) but it back-fired in a big way.

Thinking that beautiful Sarah was unattached, King Abimelech had her brought to his palace to be his wife. God was having none of that. He showed up in a dream and warned the king that he'd made a mega mistake and because of that he was going to die. Abraham was God's key man and no one messed with his wife.

Abimelech protested his innocence and said that he had no idea Sarah was married to Abraham. The king was frightened for his life and returned Sarah to Abraham mega quick, like God had told him to.

Take a look in Bible book Genesis, chapter 20 and have a read of verses 14 to 16 to see what else King Abimelech did to try to get back into God's good books.

41

MIRACLE MAKER

I t's one thing to create something if you've got the stuff to make it with, but imagine making a clay pot without any clay or, for that matter, a cake without any ingredients. That would be weird, wouldn't it? It would also be impossible – but not for someone like God.

When God made the universe in which we live (including planet Earth and everything on it), guess what He had to make it with? You're right! Nothing. Zilch! The Bible says that before the universe was made there was just God. That was it. Nothing else, just Him. Now at this point you're going to need to take my advice and try not to work it out. If you do there's every chance that your brain will overload and explode, and that's just going to be plain old messy. Take the Bible's word for it and listen to how it happened.

For starters, at the very beginning it was pitch black. If people had been around (which they weren't) they wouldn't have been able to see their hands in front of their faces. So how did God create light? Simple. He commanded it to come into being. In fact, that's how everything was created – by God telling it to exist.

When God made the world, it was completely covered in

water until He made the water separate to make way for some nice dry land. God filled the earth with all sorts of plants and animals. He put the sun in just the right place in outer space so we didn't get either fried or frozen and He even gave us the moon to be our very own night-light. How considerate is that!

Knowing how long it takes most of us to make anything, you're probably thinking that it must have taken God yonks to make everything, but think again! Head for Bible book Genesis, chapter 2 and verses 1 to 3.

42

BONKERS BABY

ere's a question for you. If God turned up at your house, would you recognise Him? That was Abraham's dilemma. One day, as he sheltered from the sweltering heat at the entrance to his tent, three men showed up. I can only guess that Abraham knew that there was something pretty special about these guys because the Bible tells us that he bowed down with his face in the dirt. Who were these VIPs? They were actually none other than God and a couple of angels, but who knows if Abraham had worked that one out yet?

Abraham insisted that the three of them stay for a bite to eat and a refreshing drink. The guests took our main man up on his offer and Abraham's wife (Sarah) set about rustling up a tasty meal for them. Now for the bombshell. One of the visitors just about blew Abraham away with the awesome news that Sarah would give birth to a son in nine months' time. What!? That's impossible, thought Abraham. He and his good lady wife were well past it (sorry to be so rude) and having a kid at their ripe old age was a ridiculous notion. Sarah was ear-wigging at the tent door and overheard what was said. She thought it was as bonkers as her hubbie and chuckled

to herself at the very thought of it. God said that nothing was too hard for Him and that when He came back in nine months' time what He had promised would have come true.

To drop in on Abraham and Sarah nine months later, head for Bible book Genesis, chapter 21 and look at verses 1 to 3.

43

SWEET (AND SOUR) DREAMS

Joseph had been banged up in prison in Egypt for something he didn't do. God looked after him and before long he was put in charge of all the other prisoners.

One day a couple of new inmates were flung into jail to join them. They were none other than the king of Egypt's wine steward and his chief baker. They'd got into the king's bad books and were now suffering as a result. One night the pair of them both had weird dreams. Nothing unusual about that you may say, but these dreams left them feeling grots. God had given Joseph the ability to interpret dreams and when Joseph offered to tell them what their unusual dreams meant they readily agreed.

The cupbearer was first to go and he told Joseph that he'd dreamt of a grapevine with three branches that blossomed and bore fruit. Then he squeezed some of the grapes into the king's cup. Joe told him that this meant that he'd be back in his old job in three days. All very encouraging. The baker perked up on hearing this and shared his dream hoping for some good news as well. He had dreamt he was carrying three bread baskets for the king. As he balanced them on his

head, birds ate from the pastries in the top basket. Sad to say, this time Joseph's interpretation wasn't quite so favourable. The baker's dream meant that in three days' time the king was going to behead him, put his head on a pole and leave it out for the birds to feed on. Yuk!

To check out if Joe was spot on with his interpretations, take a look in Bible book Genesis, chapter 40 and have a read of verses 20 and 22.

44
NOT NICE ICE

The king of Egypt (Pharaoh) was digging in his heels and refusing to release the Israelites from being his slaves. God had sent Moses to persuade him to think again, and was inflicting the land with all sorts of plagues to make Pharaoh change his stubborn mind. God could have wiped out Pharaoh and all the Egyptians in one fell swoop but He didn't.

The next plague God planned to send was the world's worst hail storm. It was going to be so destructive that He warned the Egyptians to stay indoors, and that included all their animals. Not everyone took God's helpful advice and when Moses raised his hand towards the sky and the hail began to fall it was carnage. There was thunder and lightning like you've never seen and hail so heavy that it destroyed people, animals, crops, trees and, in fact, just about everything that got in its way. As per usual, the only place that got off scot-free was Goshen where the Israelites lived. It wasn't touched.

As a result of the hail plague, Pharaoh had a temporary change of heart and called for Moses. He admitted that he'd done wrong and asked Moses, pretty please, to stop the horrid heavy hail. Moses agreed and the hail stopped at his command.

Have a guess what Pharaoh did next. Well, you don't have to. A quick peek in Bible book Exodus, chapter 9 and verses 34 and 35 will reveal all.

45

SAM'S SECRET

Who's ever heard of a man getting his strength from having long hair? Muscles, yes, but long hair, never. Well Samson, the guy who features in this Bible story, certainly did. OK, so he was a bit of a beefy fella, but the secret of his strength really came from God. His mum had dedicated him to God from birth and vowed never to cut his hair as a sign that he belonged to God. For his part, God had Samson lined up to rescue his nation (Israel) from the pesky Philistines.

Samson had a soft spot for the ladies, and when he fell head over heels in love with Delilah (a Philistine gal), the Philistine kings saw their chance to get at Samson. They offered Delilah cartloads of cash if she could just find out what made Samson so strong. Double-crossing Delilah readily agreed but it took four attempts to get Samson to share his secret.

First off, he pretended that if he was tied up with seven brand new bow strings he'd be a sitting duck for anyone who wanted to capture him. So that's what Delilah did. She had some Philistines waiting in the wings ready to nab Samson as soon as she'd tied him up. Just as they were about to seize

Israel's hero he snapped the strings as if they were threads of cotton. Delilah played all coy and hurt and tried again.

Twice more Samson played Delilah along with different answers and each time he freed himself. But Delilah wouldn't give up. She nagged and nagged until Samson cracked under the pressure and told her that it was all down to his hair. Cut that, he told her, and he'd be as weak as the next man.

To find out if Delilah earned her reward, fast forward to Bible book Judges, chapter 16 and verses 18 through to 22.

46

KRAZY KING

Rehoboam's dad (King Solomon) had died and now he'd become king of Israel. Solomon had started out really well but by the end of his reign people were glad to see the back of him. None more so than a guy called Jeroboam who'd been keeping out of the way (in Egypt) until King Solomon was off the scene. When Jeroboam found out that Solomon was dead he shot back to Israel to have a chat with Rehoboam. Jeroboam wanted to know if Israel's new king would make life easier for the people in the northern part of the kingdom who'd been given a hard time by his dad. Rehoboam wasn't going to be pushed into making a rash decision. He told Jeroboam to come back in three days and he'd have an answer for him.

First off, Rehoboam asked for the advice of the older men. Their suggestion was to give Jeroboam and the people he represented what they wanted. That way the king could guarantee their loyalty. Good thinking.

Now what did the young men who were Rehoboam's advisors have to say on the matter? Their advice was the opposite. They told the king to turn up the pressure and make life even tougher for the people of the north. Weird as it may seem, Rehoboam went along with what they had to say rather than the wisdom of the older guys.

When Jeroboam returned three days later he was shocked to be told that life was now going to be tougher, not easier, under the rule of Solomon's son.

How did Jeroboam and the people of the northern part of the kingdom take this news? Look up Bible book 1 Kings, chapter 12 and verses 16 and 17.

47

FOOD FOR THOUGHT

I f you'd lived in Israel a couple of thousand years ago you'd have had to put up with the Romans running the show. They weren't all bad, and some of them even bought into the Jewish religion. One of them, a Roman army captain called Cornelius, worshipped God and helped the Jewish poor people. God appeared to this kind man in a vision and told him to send some men to fetch a guy called Simon Peter who was staying in the seaside town of Joppa. Cornelius dispatched three of his men to go get him, and as they drew near to Joppa, Simon Peter went and had a vision of his own.

He was up on the roof praying when he got a bit peckish. While his food was being prepared for him, God served up a weird vision of a large sheet being lowered down from heaven which was choc-a-block full of all kinds of animals that Jewish people were forbidden by their law to eat. God then shocked Simon Peter by telling him to kill the animals and to eat them. Peter refused point blank, but God wasn't going to be put off that easily. God repeated the vision. In fact, he showed it to Peter three times in all just to make sure he got the message.

At that moment, Cornelius' men arrived and Simon Peter agreed to return with them to see their master. The

Jewish religion forbade Jews from visiting non-Jews (called Gentiles) but Peter now realised that God had given him the vision to show that it was all change. God wanted all people to worship Him, whoever they were and wherever they came from.

Want to discover how this story ends, then head in the direction of Bible book Acts, chapter 10 and look up verses 44 to 48.

48
ALL'S QUELL THAT ENDS QUELL

Hanging out with Jesus was always full of surprises, and you never quite knew what He was going to do next.

Jesus and His disciples were sailing from one side of the Sea of Galilee (in Israel) to another when a storm whipped up and waves began to crash over the side of the boat. Jesus' disciples were scared to death. They thought they were all going to drown. Help! But rather surprisingly, not everyone on board was biting his fingernails with worry. Jesus was actually having forty winks at the back of the boat and was oblivious to the panic going on all around Him.

His disciples woke Him from His slumber and filled Him in with what was going on. Was Jesus worried? Nope, not a bit of it. He simply got to His feet and told the wind and the waves to quit causing such a fuss, or words to that effect. And weird as it may seem, they did! The wind died down and the sea became calm. Wow!

Just to round things off, Jesus laid into His disciples for being frightened and for not trusting God.

If you want to find out what His disciples made of it all then you'll need to look up Bible book Mark, chapter 4 and read verse 41.

49

SHOT AWAY SHIMEI

Here's a weird little bit from the Bible about a guy called Shimei, who had it in for King David of Israel, big time. David was doing a runner from Jerusalem (Israel's capital city). His son, Absolom, had turned on his dad and wanted to be king in his place. How's that for gratitude? He'd rallied loads of people to get behind his treacherous plan and David was now fleeing for his life. Just in case you were concerned, King David wasn't all on his lonesome. He did have his royal bodyguard and six hundred soldiers for company as he headed out into the open countryside and away from danger. Well, almost away from danger.

Along the way, a guy called Shimei popped up. Shimei was a relative of Israel's first king (Saul), whom David had replaced, and Shimei blamed David for pushing Saul off the throne (which he hadn't) and for killing loads of Saul's family. Shimei was hopping mad and kept chucking earth and stones at King David and raining down curses on him as they went along. It was a weird sight, and one of David's men even offered to chop the head off this barmy bloke.

Did King David let him? Look up Bible book 2 Samuel, chapter 16 and verses 10 to 12 to get David's take on things.

50
TAX ATTACKS

'll tell you something for nothing. Jesus always had to have His wits about Him if He didn't want to be caught out by Israel's religious leaders. They were forever on the lookout for ways to pull Him down and ridicule Him. The good news was that Jesus was far too sharp to ever let that happen. He was always at least one step ahead of the game and most times the religious leaders ended up with egg on their faces. That's what's going on in this Bible story.

Jesus and His disciples (the bunch of guys who went around with Him) were in Capernaum and that day it was the turn of the collectors of the Temple tax to see if they could get one over on God's Son. All Jewish men over the age of twenty had to fork out half a shekel each year as their contribution towards the day-to-day running costs of God's Temple in Jerusalem.

The Temple tax collectors in this story wanted to check whether Jesus paid His taxes, and if He didn't, He'd be breaking their law. Sneaky! Peter stood up for Jesus and said that of course He'd pay, but here's where the weird bit happens. Jesus didn't fish around in a purse for the right change but He did tell Peter to do a bit of fishing for a shekel that would cover both their taxes.

Intrigued? Go to
Bible book Matthew,
chapter 17 and look
up verse 27.

NATIONAL DISTRIBUTORS

UK: (and countries not listed below)
CWR, Waverley Abbey House, Waverley Lane, Farnham, Surrey GU9 8EP.
Tel: (01252) 784700 Outside UK (44) 1252 784700 Email: mail@cwr.org.uk

AUSTRALIA: KI Entertainment, Unit 21 317-321 Woodpark Road, Smithfield,
New South Wales 2164. Tel: 1 800 850 777 Fax: 02 9604 3699
Email: sales@kientertainment.com.au

CANADA: David C Cook Distribution Canada, PO Box 98, 55 Woodslee Avenue,
Paris, Ontario N3L 3E5. Tel: 1800 263 2664 Email: sandi.swanson@davidccook.ca

GHANA: Challenge Enterprises of Ghana, PO Box 5723, Accra.
Tel: (021) 222437/223249 Fax: (021) 226227 Email: ceg@africaonline.com.gh

HONG KONG: Cross Communications Ltd, 1/F, 562A Nathan Road, Kowloon.
Tel: 2780 1188 Fax: 2770 6229 Email: cross@crosshk.com

INDIA: Crystal Communications, 10-3-18/4/1, East Marredpalli, Secunderabad –
500026, Andhra Pradesh. Tel/Fax: (040) 27737145
Email: crystal_edwj@rediffmail.com

KENYA: Keswick Books and Gifts Ltd, PO Box 10242-00400, Nairobi.
Tel: (020) 2226047/312639 Email: sales.keswick@africaonline.co.ke

MALAYSIA: Canaanland, No. 25 Jalan PJU 1A/41B, NZX Commercial Centre, Ara
Jaya, 47301 Petaling Jaya, Selangor. Tel: (03) 7885 0540/1/2
Fax: (03) 7885 0545 Email: info@canaanland.com.my

Salvation Publishing & Distribution Sdn Bhd, 23 Jalan SS 2/64, 47300 Petaling Jaya,
Selangor. Tel: (03) 78766411/78766797 Fax: (03) 78757066/78756360
Email: info@salvationbookcentre.com

NEW ZEALAND: KI Entertainment, Unit 21 317-321 Woodpark Road, Smithfield,
New South Wales 2164, Australia. Tel: 0 800 850 777 Fax: +612 9604 3699
Email: sales@kientertainment.com.au

NIGERIA: FBFM, Helen Baugh House, 96 St Finbarr's College Road, Akoka, Lagos.
Tel: (01) 7747429/4700218/825775/827264 Email: fbfm_1@yahoo.com

PHILIPPINES: OMF Literature Inc, 776 Boni Avenue, Mandaluyong City.
Tel: (02) 531 2183 Fax: (02) 531 1960 Email: gloadlaon@omflit.com

SINGAPORE: Alby Commercial Enterprises Pte Ltd, 95 Kallang Avenue #04-00, AIS
Industrial Building, 339420. Tel: (65) 629 27238 Fax: (65) 629 27235
Email: marketing@alby.com.sg

SOUTH AFRICA: Struik Christian Books, 80 MacKenzie Street, PO Box 1144,
Cape Town 8000. Tel: (021) 462 4360 Fax: (021) 461 3612
Email: info@struikchristianmedia.co.za

SRI LANKA: Christombu Publications (Pvt) Ltd, Bartleet House, 65 Braybrooke
Place, Colombo 2. Tel: (9411) 2421073/2447665 Email: dhanad@bartleet.com

USA: David C Cook Distribution Canada, PO Box 98, 55 Woodslee Avenue, Paris,
Ontario N3L 3E5, Canada. Tel: 1800 263 2664 Email: sandi.swanson@davidccook.ca

CWR is a Registered Charity – Number 294387

CWR is a Limited Company registered in England – Registration Number 1990308

More of Andy Robb's colourful Bible stories with crazy cartoons and cliff-hanger endings, to stop you getting bored!

50 Goriest Bible Stories

A sword plunged to the hilt into a super-fat king's blubber, a bloke getting killed by lightning, cold-blooded murder, tons of people drowning, scary skin diseases, famines, earthquakes! Ready to be grossed out? Jump in!

ISBN: 978-1-85345-530-8

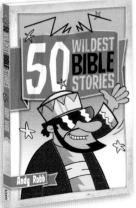

50 Wildest Bible Stories

A slippery serpent suggested sin, a bunch of builders babbled away, a pair of past-it parents produced a baby, angels ate with a guy called Abe, bad boys became bear bait! Looking for a really wild time? Tuck in!

ISBN: 978-1-85345-529-2

50 Craziest Bible Stories

Some crazy things happened in the Bible like the stories of Jonah and the big fish, Elijah and the prophets of Baal, Balaam and the donkey, the feeding of the 5,000, and Jesus' resurrection. Go on - get ka-rayzee!

ISBN: 978-1-85345-490-5

For current prices visit **www.cwr.org.uk/store**

MORE FROM ANDY ROBB

Professor Bumblebrain offers some exciting explanations, colourful cartoons and (ahem) 'hilarious' jokes answering these important questions:

Who is God? What is He like?
Where does He live?
How can I get to know Him?
ISBN: 978-1-85345-579-7

Who's the bravest? Who's the funniest? Who's the jammiest? Who's the strongest?
ISBN: 978-1-85345-578-0

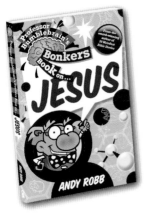

Who is Jesus? Where did He come from? What was His mission?
What's it to me?
ISBN: 978-1-85345-623-7

Who made the universe? How old is planet earth? What about dinosaurs? Was there really a worldwide flood?
ISBN: 978-1-85345-622-0

Get into God's Word

Topz is a popular bimonthly devotional for 7- to 11-year-olds.

The Topz Gang teach children biblical truths through daily Bible readings, word games, puzzles, riddles, cartoons, competitions and simple prayers.

Available as individual issues or as a year's subscription (six issues)

YP's is a dynamic bimonthly devotional for 11- to 15-year-olds.

Each issue is packed with cool graphics, special features and articles, plus daily Bible readings and notes for two months.

Available as individual issues or as a year's subscription (six issues)

For current prices visit **www.cwr.org.uk/store**

Danny's Daring Days

Talented footballer Danny learns how to step out in faith, believing that God and His love will always be with him.

ISBN: 978-1-85345-502-5

John's Jam-Packed Jottings

John learns about loyalty to Jesus and God's forgiving nature.

ISBN: 978-1-85345-503-2

Josie's Jazzy Journal

Josie, with the help of best friend Sarah, learns how to show God's love.

ISBN: 978-1-85345-457-8

Paul's Potty Pages

Paul from the Topz Gang tries to impress the new American girl in his class, with disastrous results!

ISBN: 978-1-85345-456-1

Benny's Barmy Bits

Discover with Benny how God wants to be the most important part of our lives.

ISBN: 978-1-85345-431-8

Sarah's Secret Scribblings

Join Sarah from the Topz Gang as she learns to pray for people who upset her, discovers that everyone is special to God, and more.

ISBN: 978-1-85345-432-5

Dave's Dizzy Doodles

Dave discovers it's never too late for God to turn things around.

ISBN: 978-1-85345-552-0

Gruff & Saucy's Topzy-Turvy Tales

Gruff and Saucy learn that, although it's sometimes hard trying to live God's way, He gives us the Holy Spirit to help us.

ISBN: 978-1-85345-553-7

For current prices visit **www.cwr.org.uk/store**